Five Element Chi Kung
Just Makes You Feel Good

Contents

Foreword

If you are in any doubt about practising the exercises in this book it is best to consult your doctor before proceeding.

Let me say before we start that I am a man of few words - I don't like to use one hundred words when ten will do, therefore I have tried to make explanations of these exercises easier with the aid of photographs.

Why am I so passionate about Chi Kung and Tai Chi? –The simple answer is I know they work and they can work for you too!!!

Over the last 30 years or more, these exercises have helped me through some difficult physical and emotional times - I should emphasise here that neither Chi Kung or Tai Chi can be learned solely from a book or DVD etc. You do need someone to correct your postures and the way that you move because the chances are that what you think you are doing and what you are actually doing are two different things!!!

This book will concentrate on the practice of 5 Element Chi Kung and I hope that by explaining the principles and concepts of the art as well as sharing some of my favourite exercises you will feel encouraged to find a class and begin your own personal journey, for that is what Chi Kung is, a journey and we have to accept that there may be no destination – just enjoy the ride and scenery!!!

5 Element Chi Kung

What is it and how does it work?

5 Element Chi Kung works on the theory of Traditional Chinese Medicine using static and moving exercises/meditations to open and relax the joints and muscles to allow greater energy (Chi) flow through the meridians and organs of the body.

The five elements are Earth, Metal, Water, Wood and Fire and each element relates to a pair of organs in the body (one Yin and one Yang – for example, Metal relates to Lungs (Yin) and Large Intestine (Yang) – each element relates to an emotion, colour, direction, taste, sound and animal (see chart for breakdown).

The elements work in a support cycle where each element feeds the next and a control cycle where one would control another should it be out of balance.

The Support Cycle   **The Control Cycle**

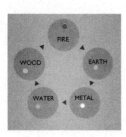   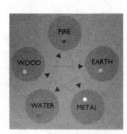

For the purpose of this book we will be working on the support cycle as there are many reasons that a particular element may be out of balance and our primary purpose is to keep a well balanced system.

<u>Lets Get Started!</u>

During these pages I will refer to certain points or techniques which you may not know so here is a brief explaination.

<u>Kidney One</u>

Kidney one is situated about the centre of the foot and it is the point where you want to feel the majority of your weight going through to the floor with a good connection to earth - This spot is also an excellent acupressure point if you feel that you require grounding and is the beginning of the kidney meridian.

<u>Pericardium Eight</u>

Pericardium Eight is found at the centre of the palm – if you trace a line from the tip of the middle finger (end of Pericardium meridian) down through the centre of the hand you will find it! It is a very powerful point and the focus of sending out healing energy.

The Tiger's Mouth

The Tiger's Mouth is formed by opening the thumb and forefinger thus encouraging energy flow through the lung and large intestine meridians. The lung meridian ends in the thumb and the large intestine starts in the index finger. The Tiger's Mouth is prominent in metal element exercises

Ban Hui Point

The Ban Hui point is the crown of the head or where you would find the 'Soft Spot' on a newborn baby!!! When we stand we feel this spot lifting (as if suspended from above) and connecting to the 'heaven' energy. When the Ban Hui point is lifted and the 'tailbone' is dropped you should feel a very subtle, pleasant stretch in the spine.

The Perineum

This is the point between the anus and the scrotum and it is the connection to the governing and conception energy channels. The governing channel runs up the back of the body and deals with the immune and nervous system and the conception channel runs down the front of the body and deals with the internal organs.

Abdominal Breathing

When you breathe abdominally your abdomen expands as you inhale and contracts as you exhale. This helps the diaphragm to work well and prevents shallow breathing. Shallow breathing is a sure sign of tension in the body and once you can master abdominal breathing you will find it easier to relax. It is important that you do not force the abdomen in and out - the breath should feel natural and calm. If you have trouble with this the best thing to do is release the shoulders and give a little sigh to relax and slightly sink the chest.

Wu Ji

We always start our sessions or return to Wu Ji between exercises. Wu Ji is stillness - Wu Ji will be looked at in more depth when we look at the exercises.

5 Element Chart

Each element is responsible for a pair of organs - one Yin and one Yang and also relates to a season, direction, colour, sound, emotion and taste. The table below shows these characteristics more clearly.

	Earth	metal	water	wood	fire
Yin organ	spleen	lungs	kidneys	liver	heart pericardium
Yang organ	stomach	large intestine	bladder	gallbladder	small intestine triple burner
season	late summer	autumn	winter	spring	summer
Direction	Central	West	north	East	South
colour	yellow/brown	white	blue	green	red
climate	dampness	dryness	cold	wind	heat
sound	singing	weeping	groaning	shouting	laughter
emotion	worry	grief	fear	anger	joy
taste	sweet	pungent	salty	sour	bitter
animal	monkey	tiger	bear	deer	crane
orifice	lips	nose	ears	eyes	face

<u>Yin Yang Symbol and Meaning</u>

The Yin Yang symbol shows us the constant interaction between these two forces. The dark part of the symbol (Yin) reaches its peak before sliding into the light (Yang) side of the symbol. The two small circles within the larger segments remind us that there is always Yin within Yang and vice versa - neither can exist without the other. A good example of this is the sun and moon - at the middle of the day when yang (the Sun) is at its highest the moon cannot be seen, but of course it is there waiting to bring the softness of the night - the interaction between Yin and Yang. We couldn't have life on Earth without this wonderful interaction.

See Chart below for Yin/Yang qualities. Notice that as energy they are neither good or bad. There are many examples of Yin and Yang apart from those shown - how many can you think of?

Yin	**Yang**
Dark	Light
Moon	Sun
Female	Male
Soft	Hard
Winter	Summer
Left	Right
Cold	Heat
Night	Day
Stillness	Movement

Explaining the Elements

Earth

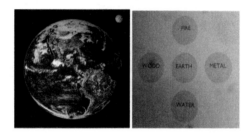

As you can see from the above chart Earth's Direction is Central. If you look at a compass it will be the pin that holds the needle or if you think of it as a wheel it would be the Hub that holds spokes together. Earth ensures the smooth transaction between one element and another and between the seasons.

Earth nurtures and holds the space, harmonising yin and yang allowing growth. Another characteristic is stillness which can be found in Wu Ji and that special place where your breath turns around or that central space between yin and yang. Imbalances of the Earth element are seen when someone is worried or anxious, they may also crave sweet foods. they may suffer from mouth ulcers or tiredness after eating or general fatigue. A good Earth element builds trust and a good sense of grounding and stillness.

A basic explanation of imbalance of Earth would be that if it is deficient then it is not being fed by its mother (Fire) and an excess would mean it is not being controlled by Wood but this is a very simplistic explanation and the reasons can be much more complex - it is for that reason we are concentrating on the support cycle.

Metal

Metal is often represented as a crystal because metal can come in various forms - it can be solid but can be liquid when heat is introduced and for this reason fire is the controller of metal whereas the supporter is Earth.

We see from the table that Metal relates to the Lungs and Large Intestine and the emotion behind it is grief - this doesn't have to be grief as in mourning a death but can be anything from choosing a wrong partner or career path. An imbalance of the Metal element can come out through the skin as eczema or through the lungs as asthma or even through the nose with excess mucus - diarrhoea or constipation are also symptoms of imbalance. When the emotion is extreme and not recognised or dealt with the outcome can be more severe as in cancers etc. Sometimes you may not even be aware that you are holding grief, or if you are you may not know what it is! Metal workshops often bring on tears once the emotion comes to the forefront of your attention and tears are a way of releasing the feeling - never be afraid to cry. It is one of our most beneficial outlets for our emotions.

A good metal element will bring balance, clarity and integrity into your life - you will know how and where to set your boundaries.

<u>Water</u>

Water, like metal, is a Yin element and the most powerful of all. It has the ability to find the lowest point and take the easy path (going with the flow). It can be still or a raging torrent. Like metal it can come in many forms, ice or steam but it always has the ability to transform back to water. Metal is the mother of Water and Earth the controller. The time of year for Water is winter when everything is still - trees have sent their energy deep into the earth waiting for the emergence of spring, some animals hibernate using the energy they have gathered through the year to sustain them during this time of rest.

Water relates to the Kidneys (Yin) and Bladder (Yang) and the emotion of fear. Water imbalance can show itself through lower back and knee pain but also through ear and urinary problems. It is also closely connected to our reproductive system so other symptoms could be prostate problems, impotence or infertility. A person with a Water imbalance will appear fearful, have very low self esteem and also have a tendency to depression. A person with a good Water element will be confident (not arrogant), outgoing and creative and have the ability to 'go with the flow' and not 'swim against the tide'. Wisdom is also connected to water.

<u>Wood</u>

Wood is a Yang element and relates to the Liver and Gallbladder and the emotion behind it is anger but on the positive side someone with a good Wood element will be very creative and kind. Wood is all about growth and spirals so lots of Wood exercises involve twisting and turning.

Spring is the time of year for wood when new growth begins along with hope for the future.

Someone with an excess of Wood energy will appear very angry and must be careful not to feed this anger into the fire element where it could explode into real physical violence, even psychopathic behaviour. He will be inflexible and feel that he isn't being heard, suffer from high blood pressure and headaches whereby a deficiency could show blurred vision, cold hands and feet, passive behaviour or dry skin. Water is the mother of wood and metal is the controller therefore the theory is that for excess energy you would use metal to control and Water for deficient energy, but as mentioned earlier there can be many other complex reasons for excess/deficiency and a trip to a Traditional Chinese Medicine practitioner would be most beneficial.

Fire

Fire is a light, transforming energy - it is expansive and can purify through heat. The time of year for Fire is summer when everything is out - all our plans and creative ideas that have come from our wood element have come to fruition - someone with a good Wood element will have lots of ideas but unless it is coupled with a good Fire element then the ideas often come to nothing - how often have you had a really good idea only to see it realised by someone else (you have missed the boat). Realise that once the intention is out there it needs to materialise and if you don't do it someone else will!!!

An excess of Fire element will show itself with over excitement, inappropriate laughter, flushed face and palpitations - a deficiency will show lack of joy, disturbed dreams, cold hands and feet, no light in the eyes - I refer to this as dead eyes and lack of intention which I often notice when people practice Tai Chi forms.

Once again in theory if there is a deficiency in the Fire element it is because it isn't being fed by its mother Wood and if in excess it isn't being controlled by Water.

A person with a balanced Fire element will be ordered and confident and be happy and light in disposition.

A Resume of the Five Elements

So, above are the main characteristics of the five elements. I haven't gone into tremendous detail because there are many books on the subject and one that I really recommend is 'Wood becomes Water' by Gail Reichstein - this is one of the textbooks used while training with the College of Elemental Chi Kung in London.

You may also notice that some characteristics are common in one or two of the elements - for instance, high blood pressure can be seen in Wood and Fire elements, diarrhoea and constipation can be a symptom in all of them therefore it is essential that on a basic level we work to balance the elements with our training - it is not the intention of this book to go into the complex issues of Traditional Chinese Medicine.

For the elements to be well balanced other factors of life also need to be looked into - Chi is taken into our body in two ways; through the air we breathe and the food we eat therefore train in as clean environment as you can - preferable outside amongst nature, if this is not possible have a space that emanates calm and stillness - your own quiet place where you can have time to yourself. You need to train everyday to attain maximum benefits of Chi Kung - often when I say this to people they say they don't have time and if I advise them to get up a little earlier they look at me as if I have asked them to go and find the holy grail!!!

Food - try and eat fresh vegetables, preferably organic and in season - if you feel the need to eat meat then once again organically reared is best. Personally, I feel there is a lot of 'fear' energy taken in when eating meat - you just have to see animals being taken to the abattoir to know this is so. I used to love eating lamb but one day I was on holiday in Scotland practising some Chi Kung outside when I became aware of eyes on me and then two lambs were rubbing round my legs and that was that - no more lamb for me!!! I very rarely eat meat these days and never partake of red meat - I find this can play havoc with the digestive system (probably for the reason given about 'fear' energy).

The Chinese say that if you practice Chi Kung consecutively for a hundred days you will see a profound improvement in your health and well being and I believe this to be correct so let's go on and practice some of my favourite standing, moving and meditation exercises to start you off on your journey.

Lets Begin with Wu Ji

Wu Ji is the way we begin and end all of our sessions.

Wu Ji is a state of stillness - the point where nothing is moving - the point before Yin and Yang begin to form. When in position you will feel your body making adjustments to posture and breathing - these adjustments will be subtle but at the same time dynamic - it may be the first time you are truly aware of your body.

To begin, stand with your feet shoulder width apart and parallel (toes pointing forward) - your knees follow the direction of the toes - do not let them drop in as this can cause knee problems later and may even be the reason for some of your knee problems now!!! Allow the weight to evenly distribute down through the pelvis and legs (do not favour one side or compensate for problems you may already have in posture). Relax the knees and feel the tailbone drop slightly causing a slight stretch in the lower back. Let the shoulders relax and arms find their place at the side of the body. Feel the rib cage relax and pressure on the internal organs start to ease. The crown of the head rises as if being suspended from above creating a subtle stretch throughout the whole of the spine.

Breathe abdominally and note how the spine starts to adjust along with the rest of the body - take mental notes of any feelings of discomfort or blockages in the meridians.

Keep this posture for about 5 mins.

See photos for right and wrong postures.

Fig. 1   Fig. 2   Fig. 3

Figure 1 - This posture is far too rigid causing tension in the joints and shallow breathing. Try it for yourself - how does it make you feel? Maybe tense or even slightly angry.

Figure 2 - This posture is much too floppy. We are confusing relaxation with limpness. We are talking of relaxing the mind and letting the body follow. How do you feel - lethargic, even slightly depressed! Return to Wu Ji and feel the energy return.

Figure 3 - This posture is correct - Just right - weight evenly spread through the legs and pelvis - arms relaxed at the side - chest slightly sunk to allow abdominal breathing - shoulders relaxed and head supported from above.

If you have any doubts about these postures try standing rigid as if to attention - how does that feel - then just let the body drop into Wu Ji naturally - the difference is amazing.

The Opening Exercise

This is the exercise we often start our Chi Kung sessions with and is one of my very favourites to practice. It opens the joints and relaxes the muscles and massages the internal organs.

Position one

Sit with the soles of the feet together with the hands holding the toes - let your knees find their own place - do not try to force them down. Relax the shoulders and breathe abdominally while focusing on the body.

Position two

Stretch the right foot out to the side and let the sole of the left foot come to the inside of the right thigh. Let the left arm rest gently on the left knee allowing the pelvis to open a little further. Make sure the back is straight and you are breathing abdominally – relax with the posture – hold for at least one minute

Position Three

Bring the left hand up so that it dangles in front of the forehead – Palm out – lift the elbow and turn the head towards the elbow. As you lean to the right the right lung compresses and the left lung opens. Once again hold this position for at least a minute.

Positions Four and Five

Repeat positions two and three with left leg extended and right leg tucked.

Position 6

Bring the soles of the feet together, hold the toes and let the head drop so that you feel a stretch along the spine. The spine is now curved   with a feeling of space between the vertebrae. This position benefits the heart and small intestine.

Position 7, 8, 9 and 10

Leaving the left leg in front of the body bring the right leg round to form a right angle. Place the hands in front of the body and slowly make your way round until you have a hand either side of the left knee then slide forward so that the stomach and spleen are squashed on the left leg. (hold for one minute). Draw the hands back, place your left forearm flat on the floor and then send the right hand back opening the chest. Hold for 1 minute and then bring the hand back to the side of the knee and keeping as low as possible while making your way back to the centre and push up. Repeat on the right side squashing the liver and gallbladder and opening the chest.

Position 11

Repeat position six.

Position 12 and 13

As you sit up, slide the hands under the legs, palms facing outwards and sit back balancing on the coccyx. Keep relaxed. Hold for about 1 min and then cross the legs and hold under the feet again for approx. 1 min.

Final Position

Sit quietly for a few minutes scanning the body, noticing how you are feeling and observing your breath.

For maximum benefit repeat three rounds of this exercise.

This is an excellent exercise to repeat several times - you will really feel a difference in the joints and muscles and the internal organs will feel soft and energised.

Earth Static and Moving Exercises

In this first exercise we are looking to make contact with the Earth energy through our pericardium 8, kidney 1 and perineum points (refer to earlier chapter to see these points) - the idea here is to feel grounded with a feeling of stillness. Stand feet shoulder width apart - weight evenly distributed, knees relaxed and spine straight. Turn the palms down. This posture gives a feeling that everything is ok and we have no worries or anxiety. While holding the posture make sure that your shoulders are relaxed and you are breathing abdominally - you will more than likely feel the feet rooted to the floor, so much so that they may even ache and you may find the sensation of the P8 points actually in contact with the floor, feeling as if you were to push down you would push yourself up!!! The Perineum also connects to the floor making the posture stable.

After standing in the static posture for 2 minutes (longer if you feel comfortable) bring the hands into the centre and turn the palms outwards - from there, breathe in taking the arms out to the side while at the same time rising. Turn the palms inwards and while breathing out sink and draw the hands in. It is important that you coordinate your movement with your breath taking particular notice of the space of no breath while you are turning your hands. This is the transitional time between Yin and Yang. The movement itself brings a feeling of calmness - do not try and breathe too slow or the moves will feel wooden and stiff. Try to keep a direct connection to your lower dan tien feeling as if you are opening and closing from that area. My own visualisation when doing this is that of a cord attached to the dan tien and pericardium 8 points feeling a stretch as I pull out and a drawing in as I breathe out and bring the hands in - you can make up your own visualisation - anything that works for you best. You may find that by opening the fingers as the hands go out and close them as they come in you get a real feeling of expansion and contraction.

Wise Monkey Turns His Head

This is one of my favourite Earth exercises and an ideal way to understand the coordination of breath and movement and remaining grounded.

Begin by standing in Wu Ji and then bring the hands in so the palms face and connect to the lower Dan Tien. After a minute or so, breathe in, rise and begin to open the arms to the side while turning the head to the left. Breathing out the hands return to lower Dan Tien while the head returns to the centre - sink back from the centre as you do this.

Repeat to the other side.

While practising this exercise ensure your movements coordinate with the breath.

<u>Regulate Stomach and Spleen</u>

This is one of the first Earth exercises I learned - not only does it benefit the stomach and spleen but also the liver and gallbladder and lungs.

1) Cross the hands in front of the body (right hand furthest away)

2) Inhale as you separate the hands - right hand rises (palm up) left hand drops (palm down)

3) Turning the body to the left, hold the breath and stretch up and down - the head looks behind.

4) Breathing out, return to the centre allowing the left hand to rise, finishing furthest from the body.

Repeat sending the left hand up etc.

Repeat at least 3 times either side.

Always turn in the direction of the lower hand.

Metal Static and Moving Exercises

Fig. 1   Fig. 2   Fig. 3

This static posture (Figure 1) is called 'The Bell' - the hands are in the 'Tiger's Mouth' position (see figure in earlier chapter) - Once again feel a good connection to Earth through the Kidney 1 spots while the elbows are loose and the index finger (Large Intestine Meridian) points to the ground. Imagine you are actually standing in a bell - feel the circle of the bell all around you giving the feeling of protection and boundaries which are two of the characteristics of the Metal element. You should feel a definite difference between this posture and the Earth posture earlier. As in all of the static postures let the body be relaxed especially around the shoulders and pelvis. Hold this position until you feel a good connection before moving on to the moving part of the exercise.

From the standing posture, inhale while bringing the hands up to shoulder height (Figure 1) the hands still in Tiger's Mouth position and palms upward - rise as you do this turning the thumbs backwards.

Exhale, sinking bring the hands down to lower dan tien, index fingers pointing downwards. (Figure 3)

Continue for at least two minutes coordinating movements with the breath before returning to the bell posture.

This is a very powerful exercise - remember that Metal relates to the Lungs and Large Intestine and the emotion of grief - while you are opening the arms you are acknowledging grief that you may be holding in the lungs and when the hands come down to the lower position you are releasing through the Large Intestine. You may become very tearful when you do this exercise but it is all part of the process!!!

The Archer

This exercise has all the characteristics of a metal exercise - opening the tiger's mouth and contracting and releasing the muscles. I really like this exercise.

Begin by standing with feet about a shoulder width and a half apart (Figure 1) - more if you feel comfortable. Make sure your back is straight with a good connection to heaven and earth. Push hands out to the side (In Tiger's Mouth position), index finger pointing up. Hold the position for at least one minute.

Fig 2. Exhale and sink drawing in the elbows making fist while contracting the muscles (pull in as much as you can) - make sure the move down is a squat and not a bend from the waist. Hold for a few seconds.

Figure 3 - As you rise, inhale and relax the body while pulling back the left arm as if drawing a bow - the hand is formed into a light fist - the right hand pushes out pulling back the index finger to open up the lung/large intestine channel.

Breathing out, sinking and contracting again as in Fig 2.

Relax, breathing in this time drawing the bow in the opposite direction as in Fig 3.

Breathing out, sink and contract once more (See Fig 2)

Repeat for several rounds and then as you breathe in, relax and push both hands out to the side once again as in Fig 1.
Hold for approx. 1 minute breathing naturally before returning to Wu Ji.

Developing Wei Chi

Wei Chi is the protective layer that surrounds us - it defines our boundaries and protects us from infection. This exercise helps us to build Wei Chi and also dispel stale Wei Chi. When our Wei Chi is weak, problems often show themselves on the skin (eczema) or lungs (asthma). We may also be prone to colds and chest infections. Wei Chi helps to boost our immune system.

Stand with feet just over a shoulder width apart, knees relaxed and back straight. Bring the hands up in front of the body with the thumbs and forefingers pointing to each other. Feel a connection as if the energy is flowing around in a circle in front of you; at the same time be aware of the space you are holding. This posture should feel very protective. Hold for 2 mins - more if comfortable.

Rise while opening the arms and then sink back down only this time with your palms facing outwards as if making a definite boundary. Make a connection to the outside - once again this posture should feel very protective - hold the posture for at least 2 mins - more if comfortable.

As you rise slightly, let the arms stretch in front of you and then bring them back so that the Pericardium 8 points cover the Lung 1 and 2 points. This is the only time the palms will touch the body for the duration of this part of the exercise. Breathe in and rise slightly while at the same time open the fingers as you draw the hands out about six inches from the body. Sinking down, breathing out, closing the fingers, drawing the hands back (do not make contact with the body though). The opening and closing of the fingers give a definite feeling of drawing out and pulling in. I often liken this to thinking of a cord being drawn in and out of a hoover or something like that.

After a few minutes of opening and closing on Lung1 and 2 rise and while inhaling let the arms open out let them rest on top of each other behind the back. breathe out and sink back down. Try and feel the breath actually working around this area - if you are breathing abdominally it sends the breath around the back automatically. Hold this position for a couple of minutes.

Bring the arms to the front of the body - hands in the 'Tiger's Mouth' position with the backs of the hands facing each other. When in this position visualise stale Wei Chi dropping to the floor from the index fingers which are pointing to the ground. The sensation of this posture is very strong - you may feel that the index fingers are swollen and much bigger than normal or a strong pulse may be felt in the fingertips.

On completion of the exercise return to Wu Ji and brush off the body dispelling any stale Wei Chi that may remain.

Water Static and Moving Exercises

Stand with feet shoulder width apart - weight evenly distributed through the feet - bring the hands (palms down) parallel to the floor around the height of the kidneys. Below the waist should feel grounded and settled into the floor - imagine you are standing in a lake and the feet are secure in the earth beneath you. The hands feel like they are floating on the top of the water making the upper body feel light and supple. Stand in this posture for several minutes.

<u>Water Shower!</u>

Stand feet shoulder width apart and hold the hands in front of the Dan Tien palms up.

Inhaling, lift the hands up the centre of the body slowly turning the palms so that when they are above the head they face upwards with the fingertips facing. Simultaneously you are rising and looking up.

Exhaling, turn the palms to face the body slowly bringing the hands down. Visualise cool water running down the front of the body as you do this. Repeat several times.

This exercise is very calming and grounding.

<u>Water (Sea Form)</u>

This exercise is designed to emulate the ebb and flow of the tide.

Begin with all the weight in the back foot and place the other foot forward - the hands are drawn back to the shoulders with the wrist relaxed - the back foot is at 45 degrees and the front foot points straight ahead.

As you exhale shift the weight into the front leg while dropping the wrist and pushing forward - do not over extend.

Inhale and drawback, exhale and push forwards.

Repeat several times and then change to the other side.

Coordinate your movement with the breath and keep the movement smooth and flowing while becoming aware of the shift of weight from one leg to the other.

This exercise is calming and grounding while at the same time generating strength and power.

<u>Wood Static and Moving Exercises</u>

<u>Wood (Cycle of a Tree!)</u>

Fig. 1   Fig. 2   Fig. 3

Fig. 4   Fig. 5   Fig.6

Fig. 7   Fig. 8

This exercise emulates the life cycle of a tree from Summer (opening the arms), Autumn (bringing the arms back), Winter (drawing the hands in and pushing down as if taking sap down for the winter months), Spring (drawing the energy up and down the liver channel - twice) and then back to summer. As you familiarise yourself with the exercise you may find you rise and fall as you do this sequence.

Fig. 1 - From Wu Ji bring the hands up to the front of the body and as if you are actually hugging a tree - the knees are unlocked and the body straight (tailbone dropped and crown of the head drawn up). Hold this position for two minutes.

Fig. 2 - As you inhale, open the arms wide - visualise the tree in full leaf,

Fig. 3 - Exhale while bringing the hands back to Fig. 1 position representing the end of summer and bringing the energy in for Autumn.

Figs. 4 and 5 - Inhale while drawing the hands back towards the chest - turn the palms and exhale while pushing the hands down - this represents taking the tree's energy (sap) down for the Winter.

Figs 6 and 7 - As you inhale, draw the hands up the liver channel at the front of the body to the eyes then turn the palms, exhale and take the hands back down - repeat this movement once more. This represents Spring and the wood element.

Fig. 8 - Inhale, open the arms back to Fig. 2 position and begin the sequence again - repeat at least 5 times to feel the full benefit of the exercise - On completing your final sequence return to hugging tree posture for 2 mins then return to Wu Ji.

<u>Wood (Spiralling)</u>

Wood exercises often involve spiralling movements and this exercise really emphasises this. When you practise this feel the back and chest opening and closing as you do the spiralling movements. How does it feel as you bring the spiral in - feel the difference as you open up the spiral. Wood exercises work on opening the joints and toning the muscles of the body

Fig. 1   Fig. 2   Fig. 3   Fig. 4

To begin this exercise from Wu Ji, move into the wood standing posture - knees relaxed, back straight, weight evenly distributed, hugging the tree. (Fig. 1)

Fig. 2 - Exhale spiralling the right arm up and left arm down. Do not let the shoulders lift, let the elbows draw in to help create the feeling of the back opening and the chest closing - both palms face outward and the arms are on the centre line.
As you inhale, let the arms return to the original wood position. The chest is now open (Fig. 3) .

Fig. 4 - Exhale and repeat spiral with left hand rising and right hand dropping - Inhale returning to Fig. 1. Repeat several times.

<u>Wood (Roots and Shoots!)</u>

This exercise creates the spiralling action of nature - as we sink and turn we have the feeling of a tap root going into the floor and as we rise we feel like a fresh shoot growing from the ground.

Fig. 1   Fig. 2   Fig. 3

Stand, feet and knees together. Palms together, forearms parallel to the floor (Fig 1)
Fig. 2 - Exhale, sink and turn to the right from the waist - try not to twist the hips. Make sure your back remains straight as you sink and the knees remain facing the front - this will give the impression of the tap root reaching into the ground.
Inhale, rise and return to Fig. 1
Fig. 3 - sink, exhale and turn to the left.

Continue for at least two minutes connecting to the sinking (Roots) and rising (shoots)

Fire (Static and Moving Exercises)

Working with Heart Dan Tien

Fig. 1   Fig. 2

From Wu Ji bring hands up to the chest with palms facing each other. (Fig 1) Relax the knees and make a connection between the Pericardium 8 points - you may feel as if you are physically holding a ball. If you have trouble making a connection then relax the shoulders. When there are problems making connections the problem usually lies in the shoulders being tense. Hold this position for at least two minutes.

When you feel a good connection point fingers forward, inhale, rise and let the hands separate. Keep the P8 points in line for as long as possible. (Fig 2) - as you exhale, sink and let the hands return to the heart (Fig. 1). Repeat the movement several times before returning to the original position. Hold for two minutes then return to Wu Ji.

<u>Opening and Closing the Chest</u>

Fig. 1   Fig. 2   Fig. 3   Fig. 4

Begin this move in Wu Ji and shift your weight to the left - turn to the right and place your right foot flat on the floor with the toes pointing forward. Inhale bringing the hands up level with the shoulders, palms up. Fig. 1. Feel the chest open.

Exhale shifting the weight forward bringing the hands to the front about shoulder width apart. Fig. 2 - You should now feel the chest close and the back open.

Repeat several times and when the weight is in the left leg and the arms open slowly turn and repeat the exercise to the other side.

When practising this exercise pay particular attention to coordinating the movement with the breath and also the shifting of the weight backwards and forwards (substantial and insubstantial and lead from the centre (Dan Tien) not with the upper body. Also ensure the palms are facing up when the weight is back to open the chest to its maximum.

<u>Resting the Heart</u>

For this exercise the heels need to be together with the toes pointing out - this is a classic fire position and used in the many of the fire element exercises especially the Crane form.

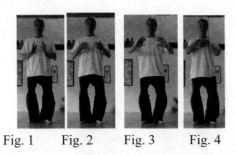

Fig. 1   Fig. 2   Fig. 3   Fig. 4

Start the exercise by making contact between the pericardium 8 points as we did in the 'Working the Heart Dan Tien' earlier but this time remember to have your 'Charlie Chaplin' foot position with the knees slightly bent going in the direction of the toes.

Fig. 2 Turn the palms inwards to make contact with the heart.

Fig. 3 Turn the palms out and slightly push away from the body making contact with the space in front of you.

Fig. 4 Turn the hands to face down with the P8 points on top of each other - the hands are connected. Visualise leaning on a staff connected to the floor. The elbows are relaxed. Feel the connection straight down to the floor.

Hold each position for at least two minutes.

Finishing your Session

Clear Excess Energy

Fig. 1   Fig. 2

Raise the hands up the sides of the body and line the pericardium 8 points up above the head (Fig. 1).

Slowly bring the hands down the front of the body visualising any excess energy rolling down the body - through the torso, pelvis and evenly down the legs and out through the feet.

Gather and Store to the Dan Tien

Fig. 1   Fig. 2

After clearing excess energy in our body we gather and store the rest into the lower Dan Tien.

Bring the hands up the sides as if collecting energy from earth and heaven (Fig. 1) and then bring the hands down the centre of the body, palms down with fingers pointing inwards (Fig. 2) and slowly bring them down the front of the body visualising energy down through the torso to the lower Dan Tien. The hands finish palms down at the height of the Dan Tien.

Repeat three times.

To conclude your session return to Wu Ji (Fig. 1) and then bring the hands to cover the lower Dan Tien - Left hand on top of the right for men and vice versa for women.

Fig. 1   Fig. 2

A common question is 'Why is the left hand on top of the right for men and vice versa for women? Well, first of all it isn't written in blood, there can be circumstances when it works the other way round!!! The general explanation is that the right side of the body corresponds to Yang and the left to Yin, therefore, if a man places his right hand on his lower Dan Tien and covers with the left this is considered Yang supported by Yin and the same explanation goes for women - left hand first (Yin) right hand on top (Yang) so it is Yin supported by Yang. However, if a man's Yang energy is too strong then it may be a good idea to stand the other way to bring some Yin energy into the body to balance things out - the same goes for women who might be too Yin thus needing a 'Yang boost'. As you become more aware of your energy you will be able to find which is best for you at a particular time.

This brings me to another interesting point - over the years I have noticed that Chi Kung classes tend to be predominantly female. Men seem to be reluctant to let go of the macho image, preferring to work out at the gym to build muscle or take up the more external martial arts which rely mostly on strength. Chi Kung itself isn't a martial art but works on the internal system allowing you to feel energy flow within the body bringing about more body awareness so if you also train in Tai Chi, which is one of the internal martial arts, it is possible to neutralise and deal with attacks very effectively. Unfortunately, when someone is too Yang they tend not to feel the need to 'soften' up so eventually the body becomes rigid and inflexible - often joints become arthritic due to energy not being able to flow freely.

On the other hand some women come along and are too Yin - this can often be seen in the eyes or posture, even the voice, sometimes there is a lack of confidence but by undertaking some Yang exercises they often bring themselves into balance finding a completely new person emerging like a butterfly from its chrysalis!

There is a Chinese saying that says 'Yin belongs to the soft and supple, Yang belongs to the rigid and dead' - It is my belief that being too Yin or too Yang are both detrimental to your physical, mental and spiritual well being but by practising Five Element Chi Kung exercises you find 'the balanced path'.

<u>Some Meditations</u>

The first meditation can be performed either sitting on a chair or
the floor, whichever is most comfortable for you - you may even
lie on your back with the arms at the side, palms up. The only
trouble with this position is that you are prone to fall asleep!
When sitting ensure that the back is straight and the head is not
slumped forward and if sitting cross legged then the knees
should be below the navel (lower Dan Tien) so it is advisable to
sit on a meditation cushion.

<u>Present moment (5 Senses) meditation</u>

Begin by focussing on the breath - take several long, deep
breaths allowing the body to relax and then let the eyes softly
focus on what you can see - it is helpful to place a candle or
crystal in front of you to give you a definite point of reference.
Stay with this for a few minutes.

Close your eyes and concentrate on your hearing. Sit with the
sounds. At first you will hear the obvious, a ticking clock or
music you may be using as an aid but as the meditation moves
on the sounds will become more subtle, maybe cars or birdsong
in the distance. Once again sit with this for a few minutes.

Move on to taste. What can you taste? As you sit with this you may find that the mouth fills with saliva and the need to swallow increases. Sit with this for a few minutes.

Next is smell - What can you smell? Take in any aromas around you; you may find this quite hard at first but keep going for at least two minutes.

Finally go to feeling. We are talking physically rather than emotional here. Any sensations in the body - feel the connection to the floor or seat, There may be a gentle breeze blowing over the skin, the palms maybe getting warm/cold. Again sit with this for a few minutes.

You will probably find you have a favourite sense, maybe even two, so to finish off the session sit with those for a few minutes before slowly returning to concentrate on the breath.

The more you practise this meditation the harder it will be for outside thoughts to intrude and a deep sense of calm will ensue.

Tree Meditation

Chi Kung, especially 5 Element Chi Kung brings us closer to nature. The more aware we become of our internal and external energy we start to feel part of the whole and not separate so for this meditation we share energy with a tree or group of trees.

To begin, respectively approach the tree/trees you would like to work with and spend a few minutes in Wu Ji.

As you inhale visualise energy rising up through the body through kidney one and out through the crown of the head - exhale visualising the energy going into the leaves and branches and down the trunk of the tree into the roots - continue this cycle for a few minutes.

Change the direction of the cycle - inhale through the crown and down through kidney one - exhale visualise the energy going through the tree's roots, up through the trunk, branches and leaves before inhaling back through the crown etc. Continue the cycle for two minutes.

I absolutely love this exercise. I particularly like to practise in the middle of a group of trees preferable evergreens like pines but I also find Oak trees really like to 'help' with this meditation - Don't forget to thank the tree before walking away.

Waterfall Meditation

Begin this meditation standing in Wu Ji until you feel
completely relaxed. Imagine standing beneath a waterfall, water
cascading down the outside of the body, cool and refreshing.
After a few minutes take your intention to the crown of the head
- imagine the water entering the body and making its way down
the spine, the arms, the legs and out through the K1 spot.
Remembering that the water element is about flow and finding
the easy route notice if you feel any points of resistance to the
flow. Release any blockages with the mind allowing the water to
find its way easily through the body.

It is a good idea on completion of this exercise to draw a
diagram of your body and mark where you found any blockages.
By doing this you can map your progress over a period of time.

These are three of my favourite meditations. I hope that you
enjoy them too.

Refreshing Head Massage

This is an excellent massage to practise any time of day when you feel tired or overworked.

1) Rub the hands together to generate heat in the palms and then take the hands around the face as if washing also running the hands over the head. You can perform this 'washing' action several times before proceeding.

2) With the palm of the hand rub backwards and forwards across the forehead erasing those wrinkles!

3) Gently push the index and middle fingers up from the base of the nose to where the eyebrows meet and back again. This helps clear the sinuses. Continue for a few minutes using gentle pressure and lots of visualisation.

4) Apply gentle pressure around the eye sockets using either the knuckle of the index finger or the tips of the fingers, whichever is most comfortable for you. Circle in both directions - next rub the hands together once more generating heat in the palms and then cup them over the eyes and feel the heat slowly penetrate the eyeballs. Once again you can perform this part of the exercise several times if you wish.

5) Using the tips of the fingers massage/tap around the mouth to improve circulation around the gums and cheeks.

6) Using the back of the hand rub vigorously under the chin - rubbing away one of those extra chins!

7) Gently massage the ear lobes with the thumb and index finger. The ears hold many acupressure points so a good massage around the outer and inner ear is really beneficial.

8) Once more rub the hands together and cup the palms over the ears with the fingers facing back so that you can tap the base of the skull. This is called beating the heavenly drum.

9) To finish the massage go back to the start giving the face and head another 'wash'.

The Three Treasures
(Jing, Chi, Shen)
Lining up the 3 Dan Tiens

The three treasures, Jing, Chi and Shen can be translated to body, mind and spirit.

Jing is the essence that we are born with and inherit from our parents and determines our development. Jing slowly diminishes through our lives and cannot be replaced, however it can be supplemented and nurtured through a healthy lifestyle. Jing resides in the kidneys and therefore affects our reproductive system. Impotence, infertility and premature ageing are all signs of Jing deficiency. When Jing energy expires, so do we!

Chi is the vital energy that drives our body and runs through the 12 meridians - good diet, regular exercise (Chi Kung), meditation, the air we breathe and regular sleep all build Chi energy and provide a good connection between our Jing and Shen.

Shen, or spirit, isn't the 'spirit in the sky' that we think of in the west but our personality, mental attitudes and spiritual development. Good Shen shines through the eyes and our demeanour. A person with good Shen will be confident but not arrogant, and be full of energy and compassion. Deficient Shen can show itself through mental disorders, sluggish behaviour and low self esteem.

There are lots of explanations for this but the easiest way I know to describe it is by comparing the three treasures to a candle. Jing, the energy which we are born with and inherit from our parents, would be the wax and wick of the candle, the main body which holds it all together. Chi, the energy that drives us would be the flame and Shen would be the halo around the flame.
Therefore the brighter the flame the more our spirit shines.

The three treasures also relate to the three dan tiens' that we work on in our Chi Kung practice - they are the lower dan tien, situated about two inches below the naval and towards the centre of the body - a good way of finding this dan tien is to place your thumb on to your naval and roll the hand down and the palm should be right on the spot. This is also around the CV6 (Conception Channel) acupressure point.

The heart or middle dan tien needs no explanation, it is in the centre of the chest at the height of the heart - this is the point that Jing and Shen amalgamate with Chi and find balance. The acupressure point often related to this dan tien is CV17.

The upper dan tien is better known as the 'third eye' - this is situated between the eyebrows and in acupressure known as GV24.5 (Governing Channel)

<u>Lining up (or balancing) the Three Dan Tiens</u>

There are several ways to balance or line up the three Dan Tiens and these are three of them. My absolute favourite which comes from the College of Elemental Chi Kung is rather complicated to be explained in photos and text so unfortunately not included here - however, these are also excellent exercises so I hope that you enjoy them.

<u>Exercise one</u>

Begin with feet shoulder width apart - the palms of the hands together with the thumbs pressing onto CV17 point.

Breathe in and slowly push hands up the centre line until you reach the top.

Breathing out slowly, lower the hands, turning the fingers down as you pass the heart. Repeat the movement several times until you feel a connection between the Dan Tiens.

Exercise Two

This exercise uses acupressure points to line up the three Dans although it is also used to relieve worry and anxiety. The exercise can be done either sitting cross legged or on a chair or standing.

Begin by sitting calmly before placing the palms together and place the fingertips on the GV24.5 point situated just between the eyebrows. This is often called the third eye. Lower the head slightly.

Bring the hands down to rest against the CV17 point at the centre of the chest with the thumbs applying a little pressure.

Turn the hands down and let the fingertips lightly press into the CV6 point about 2 inches below the naval.

Hold each position for approximately 3 minutes and then return to sitting calmly.

<u>Exercise Three</u>

This exercise is used at Master John Dings Academy of Tai Chi Chuan to settle energy at the end of each Tai Chi session but as you can see by the movements it is also balancing the 3 Dan Tiens

Stand with feet together with the hands palm up at the lower Dan Tien.

Inhale drawing the hands, palm up to the heart while at the same time lifting the heels from the floor.

Turn the palms down and while exhaling lower the hands and lower the heels.

Inhaling, raise the hands to the chest lifting the heels. Turn the palms out and push your hands forward.

Holding the breath open the hands out to the side opening the chest. Exhale and bring hands back to the centre, palms up to the Lower Dan Tien. Heels Down.

Inhale, bring the hands up the centre line pushing the hands palm up above the head at the same time raising the heels.

Push hands out to the side and exhaling let them drop, returning to the starting position. Heels down.
Repeat the sequence two more times.

After the final round stand with the right hand on top of the left and thumbs together pointing forward. (left hand on top for women).

Let your energy settle before ending your exercise.

Some Useful Acupressure Points

It is useful to have a few acupressure points 'under your belt' - they can be particularly useful when suffering from headaches, toothache, insomnia, digestive problems and can even boost your immune system when you are feeling low.

The acupressure points below are all considered power points and are easy to find. Most acupressure points are found in small dips in the skin, alongside bones and joints - Pressure is applied using the thumb or index finger but if you are not sure if you are actually on the point you can rub the general area. Some of these points (especially Large Intestine 4) are not to be used in pregnancy because they can bring on stomach cramps or even miscarriage - you should also avoid applying pressure to areas with cuts or bruising or directly onto cancerous areas.

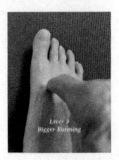

Liver 3 is an easy point to find. Follow the metatarsal bones from the big toe and first toe until they meet. Apply direct pressure - this point can be quite painful when pressed. As well as being a power point for the immune system it also relieves headaches and tired eyes and grounds the body.

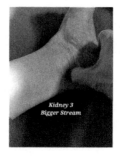

Kidney 3 is found on the inside of the foot between the ankle and the achilles tendon. As well as boosting the immune system this point also relieves fatigue, swollen feet and insomnia.

Large Intestine 11 (Crooked Pond) is found by folding the elbow and where the crease ends you will find a small indentation where you can apply pressure - once again, if you are not sure you are on the point you can massage the area.
LI11 is a power point for the immune system but can also alleviate constipation, cold and fevers and arthritic elbow pain.

Large Intestine 4 (Joining the Valley) is found by following the line from the web between thumb and index finger (following the valley) until they meet at the joint. The point is found slightly under the bone of the index finger and can be quite painful to press. Once again this is a power point used to boost the immune system but also alleviates headaches and toothache and balances the digestive system and can also help to relieve depression - **This point is not to be used during pregnancy)**.

Triple Warmer 5 (Outer Gate) This point is found approx. 3 fingers width below the wrist crease in the centre of the arm. Once again a small indentation can be found but if you are unsure if you are on the point you can rub up and down the area. This is also one of the power points for the immune system and also relieves allergic reactions and regulates and relaxes the whole body.

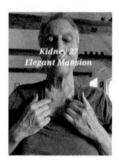

Kidney 27 (Elegant Mansion) can be a tricky point to find but it is also a power point for the immune system. If you find the protruding points of the collarbone and then come slightly down and out you will find two indentations. Rub the area if you are unsure or even tap with the fingers. K27 relieves anxiety, hiccups, sore throat and also benefits the lungs as well as the kidneys.

Bladder 23 and 47 (Sea of Vitality) is found 3 to 4 inches either side of the spine at Kidney height. I find it is much better to rub these points to generate heat in the meridian. This is a real power point for the immune system and fortifies the digestive system, relieves backache and impotency.

Stomach 36 (Three Mile Point) another power point for the immune system can be found three or four finger widths below the knee on the outside of the leg. If you place the leg flat on the floor and pull back the toes you will see a muscle 'pop up' in the area where the point is. It is called Three Mile Point because if you rub or tap these points when out walking and start to flag it is said to give you an extra three miles! It also relieves stomach disorders and nausea.

CV6 (Sea of Energy) is on the Conception Channel which runs along the front of the body from the perineum to the mouth. Relieves weakness and strengthens the lower back as well as benefiting the immune system.

CV17 (Sea of Tranquility) is another point on the conception channel and is found in the centre of the chest on the same line as the nipples. You can press with the fingertips or place the palms together and apply gentle pressure with the knuckles of the thumb. It does exactly what it says on the packet - relieves nervousness, grief, depression and emotional trauma - this point is also included in one of our lining up the Dan Tiens exercises.

Also among these power points is the Kidney one spot (Bubbling Spring) which is the area we use to ground our energy while performing Wu Ji (see Figure in 'Let's Get Started' Chapter). This point stimulates the kidneys and rejuvenates the spirit. It can also relieve feinting, impotence and epilepsy.

Of course, there are many other acupressure points along the meridians of the body but these are some of the most powerful and are well worth remembering.

The Tai Chi Studio

I opened the Studio in 2002 just after moving to Wivenhoe. At the time I worked as a London Cab Driver (hating every moment) - The original plan was to spend three days working in London and returning to Wivenhoe for the other four - this plan never materialised!!! Now cab driving isn't the cash cow that some people seem to think it is. To make a reasonable living you have to work long hours and I was never one for overwork. The time was fast approaching for the yearly 'overhaul' - this involved the cab being scrutinised by the London Carriage Office inspectors before passing it for another years roadworthiness - often this involved great expense, sometimes the bill could be well over £1000 which I was rather unwilling to pay to continue in a job I really hated, so thinking I was obviously not going to continue life as a London 'Cabbie' I decided to take the cab to the local garage for an MOT and use it as a private vehicle while deciding how I was going to make my living. The garage came back with a list as long as your arm of repairs needed to pass, I was not going to spend anymore money on this vehicle and drove to Colchester and left it with the local scrapyard - gone. I will never forget the sense of freedom felt walking back home along the Wivenhoe trail - I had absolutely no idea what I was going to do but had absolute faith, like Dickens' Mr Macawber that something would turn up.

Walking along Wivenhoe High Street I noticed several shops for rent and I thought it would be a good idea to open one but what would I do? How would I go about it? Totally unfazed by these obstacles I called the agents involved and arranged a meeting.

On meeting up with the agent she asked what sort of shop I was looking to open to which I replied that I didn't know. She looked rather puzzled at this so thinking on my feet I said maybe an art or music shop (both hobbies of mine and the only thing I could think of at the time). 'Oh,' she said. 'Have you got your business plan drawn up?' - blank look from me - big sigh from her!!!

'What else can you do?' She seemed to want to help so I told her I teach Tai Chi - I had passed my instructor course but apart from a few classes I ran in London had never really thought of going 'full time'. 'Well,' She smiled, 'I might have just the place for you' and we walked a few hundred yards to the local business centre and she showed me a unit that I immediately fell in love with. So, that was how the studio started.

One thing I have found over the years is that if you let them, things/opportunities will just unfold and this is what happened next. The Studio was becoming very popular and becoming too small so I really needed a bigger place and one Sunday morning while taking a class I happened to mention this and someone said that he ran a business centre in Great Bentley, which wasn't a million miles away and that he had a unit that might suit my needs. He was right and the Studio was on the move!!!

There followed a further, rather unsuccessful move to another site in Great Bentley which proved to be much too big!!! and impossible to heat - sadly numbers fell and it looked for a time that I would have to close altogether. However, my Great Bentley man came through again and although I could not return to my original unit in the business park there was another available which for a time saw numbers rise again - the summers were great but winters once again proved a problem and I looked around once more for a new venue.

Once again one of my students came through - her husband worked on farms and said that it would be worthwhile checking out the business centre on Hall Farm, Little Bentley which was only a few miles down the road from my current location. On speaking to the Hugh Cobbald, the farmer and owner of the site

I was told that he didn't really have anything available at the present time but did have a space that would need renovating -
He wasn't kidding, the unit was an old stable which hadn't been used in years - there was ivy growing through the walls, the floor was more or less rubble but I could see the potential straight away.
I told him that although I loved the thought of it there was no way that I could finance such a renovation - he asked what I intended to do there and when I told him and he saw my enthusiasm he offered to do everything for me, which he did without sparing the expense - of course I have probably paid him back many times now with rent (very reasonable) but I can't thank him enough - it is great, in the winter we have heating, in the summer aircon - there is a kitchen and indeed all mod cons - here is a brief history in pictures of how things progressed and as you can see the Studio isn't big, in fact, it isn't much bigger than the Wivenhoe space but small as proved to be beautiful with classes and workshops full of fun and enthusiasm.

The Transformation from Stable to Studio

About Me!

I would like to share my own personal journey with you because it's important to understand that every action and decision we make in the past has brought us to where we are - the present. Three things are certain in life - birth, death and what happens in between. We can't do much about the first and third but what we do with the 'in between' takes us on the most incredible journey. I was born in East London in 1948 in what, even then, was a multicultural society and although I was Church of England most of my friends were Jewish and I found myself becoming fascinated by their religion and culture - later in the 50's and early 60's there was a big influx of West Indian and Asian people which further fuelled my appetite to learn more about foreign cultures. Each religion had a God but each one seemed to think their God was 'The God' and everyone else was wrong. Surely this couldn't be! there was either one God or no God; I know this sounds rather naive but you have to realise I would only have been 12 or 13 at the time - I was confused but eventually found myself drawn towards the East for my spiritual direction. By the age of sixteen I was looking at Yoga (which seems to bear no resemblance to what is taught today) and reading books like The Autobiography of a Yogi - the story of Paramahansa Yogananda. All this makes me sound like a bit of a swat but that was not the case. I had girl friends, played lots of sports and enjoyed a pint like the rest.

Life changed, as it so often does in my mid twenties, I began working in the CIty of London on the Commodity Markets - this was not a good move. I wasn't suited to a fiscal career and I certainly wasn't suited to the 'drinking culture' that went with it! I hated the work and hated the people who apart from a few seemed to be preoccupied with money, cars and big houses. By the time I was 30 I was drinking too much and I guess I just wasn't a nice person to be around - My spiritual path a long distant memory. I left the City and became a London Cab Driver and embarked on another career that I absolutely hated - then destiny played its part once more, a bad knee injury stopped me taking strenuous exercise when an article in the taxi trade magazine led me to a Tai Chi school run by Master Chu King Hung in Notting HIll, London. I went along for an open evening and became hooked immediately it brought me back to 'the path' it seemed to have everything. It was a martial art but also had deep spiritual content. Zhan Zhuang Chi Kung (standing like a tree) was also part of the training and within two years my knee problem had resolved itself. Master Chu's school closed but I continued training with his top instructor before finally finding Master John Ding at the International Academy of Tai Chi Chuan where I passed to instructor level. Master Ding's understanding and transmission of Chi energy was a revelation and his teaching was open, sharing his knowledge freely although sometimes it was a bit beyond our understanding. It is only now, many years later that I sometimes realise the significance of some things that he passed on. In one of his classes we were having a general discussion about life. I was becoming more unhappy by the minute taxi driving and although I never mentioned it, Master Ding talked to us as a group and quoted Bertrand Russell who said something to the effect of 'if you don't like life, change it'. This resonated in me

and it wasn't long after that I found myself moving from
London with my family to Wivenhoe, Essex.
The Tai Chi Studio was about to be born!

   So there you have it - my journey so far and along the way
I have taught many people the benefits of both Tai Chi and Chi
Kung. Am I a Master? No, but I do consider myself a good
teacher and able to pass the knowledge I have acquired over the
years in a straightforward and easy to understand way. Some
have been with me since my early days in Wivenhoe and others
not so long but I trust that they all enjoy learning from the
classes as much as I enjoy teaching them and sharing our
journey together.

Have I finished my journey? No, lots of things in my life have
changed, but there is so much to learn and in the words of a U2
song, 'I still haven't found what I'm looking for.' Maybe I won't
until my final breath; but until then I'll continue to enjoy this
incredible ride!

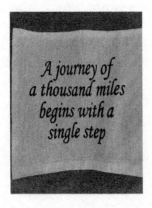

A journey of a thousand miles begins with a single step

Frequently Asked Questions

Where Can I Find a Class?

Finding a Chi Kung or Tai Chi class is quite easy. Classes seem to be popping up in every church/village hall and gymnasium and leisure centre but how do you know if they are any good? Don't be afraid to ask the instructor their background - who have they trained with? What are their qualifications? How did they come by them? How long have they been training? My advice is stay away from those who have only been training for a short while themselves or have obtained their certificates of instruction through online courses or even worse just picked up their information from books - you may laugh but this actually happens. Does your instructor 'walk the walk' and well as 'talk the talk'? It is no good if your instructor has lots of theory and no practical experience or vice versa. Realise that sometimes you may have to travel a little further than your own backyard to find an instructor of worth - do not settle for an easy option or someone who tries to rush your training. Do not be afraid to ask questions, an instructor of any worth will be proud of his/her lineage and have lots of interesting stories.

Remember that you are on a personal journey, one that you may never reach or know the destination but take your time and enjoy all the scenery along the way.

Is Chi Kung a Religion?

The simple answer is no although Chi Kung and Tai Chi are spiritual in nature. They are probably closest to Buddhism and Taoism which are more ways of life rather than religions.

What Style of Chi Kung is Best?

Like Tai Chi, Chi Kung has many styles and like Tai Chi they have their principles and concepts which remain unchanged. They all concentrate on cultivating internal energy (which is the meaning of Chi Kung) and moving energy through the meridians and like Tai Chi it may be just the exercises that differ but not the intention. Some may use static exercise (Zhan Zhuang) others may use a combination of static/moving exercises, the most important thing is a good teacher and your own dedication.

Should I learn Chi Kung or Tai Chi?

My own opinion is that it is more beneficial to begin with Chi Kung. The simple reason is that although you may think you have good body awareness, the chances are that what you think you are doing and what you are actually doing are two different things. Chi Kung builds your body awareness, improves posture and breathing and relaxation, which are also benefits of Tai Chi but the

forms in Chi Kung are much shorter than the forms of Tai Chi. Long Yang Style Tai Chi has 108 movements (there are some shorter forms), admittedly a lot of these movements are repeated while going through the form but most people find them hard to learn and remember. When I teach Tai Chi I like to make sure that the movements are remembered so that a person can practise the form on their own - going to a class and just following along with the movements give little or no benefit at all. Chi Kung exercises and forms being shorter give the beginner a better chance to connect and understand internal energy making it easier to move on to Tai Chi later.

Should I Practice Chi Kung if Pregnant?

There are definitely some areas of Chi Kung that should not be practised when pregnant but on the other hand the relaxation side of the art can be most beneficial. I know one lady who practised until the eve of the birth of her child and she found that the relaxation and breathing exercises really helped. However, there are some exercises that should not be practised specially those that work on certain acupressure points so rule of thumb would be to listen to your teacher or if your pregnancy has complications it is advisable not to train. If you are in any doubt consult your doctor.

What Initial Benefits Can I Expect From Chi Kung - How Does It Work?

Improvements in posture, breathing, relaxation, sleep patterns, digestion and overall body awareness are the main benefits to the total beginner in Chi Kung. 5 Element Chi Kung uses static and moving exercises/meditations to open and relax the joints and muscles to improve energy flow through the meridians of the body. At deeper levels you become aware of how emotions can block energy flow and affect the internal organs and using the theory of Traditional Chinese Medicine these emotions can be released bringing the body back into balance. The rate of progress depends on the individual because Chi Kung works with visualisation and intention which doesn't come easy for everyone therefore counselling could also be of benefit in relieving pent up emotions.

If you can find a Traditional Chinese Medical practitioner this can be an added bonus. Traditional Chinese Medicine treats the whole person rather than just the symptoms by using herbal remedies and acupuncture. I can tell you from experience that herbal remedies do not taste great but they work really well.

<u>How Do I remain Grounded?</u>

Some people find it difficult to remain grounded and there are various techniques you can use to help with this. If you are someone who likes to watch films of a violent nature or play violent video games this does not help with keeping grounded, in fact the opposite happens, your energy rises and you become overexcited. My advice is do not watch too much news, it is seldom good and can help bring your energy levels down -believe me if there is anything you need to know you will find out about it soon enough! Turn off your mobile phone, even for a few hours a day, if it is that important callers will leave a message - limit your time on social media and ask yourself how many of your facebook 'friends' do you really know? I bet it isn't many but most of all think positively, retain a sense of humour and just enjoy life.

Recommended Reading

You Are How You Move - Ged Sumner

Although I have studied Chi Kung with many teachers over the
years I did my teacher training at the College of Elemental Chi
Kung in London, therefore a book I recommend is 'You Are
How You Move' by Ged Sumner, co-founder of the College of
Elemental Chi Kung.
What does this mean? Well, how do you move? Are you one of
those people who walk in a confident manner or do you walk
with eyes to the ground with a sluggish gait? When you move in
a confident, not arrogant manner you feel grounded, happy in
the company of others and safe in your environment but if you
walk eyes to the floor you feel separated from the whole,
withdrawn and generally weak and insecure and this is the
message you send out to others.

**Wood Becomes Water (Chinese Medicine in Everyday Life) -
Gail Reichstein**

A really good read if you would like to know more about how
the Elements work with each other in accordance with
Traditional Chinese Medicine. The author once again keeps
things simple and easy to understand.

The Way of QiQong - Kenneth S. Cohen

This is my Chi Kung 'bible' - it has lots of information on the history of Chi Kung and also research results into the art. The book also has lots of useful exercises and meditations.

The Way of Energy - Master Lam Kam Chuen

Once again an easy to understand book - lots of information on body alignment using 'Standing Like a Tree' static exercises - there are also warming up exercises and an easy to follow 'Eight Piece of Brocade' set.

The Book of Oriental Medicine - Clive Witham

This is probably a book for the more advanced student which takes you into Traditional Chinese Medicine - it is a slightly 'harder' read than the others but it has lots of information and also a self treatment guide.

Although these books are excellent I would still like to emphasise that it is advisable to find a good teacher to set you off on your Chi Kung journey.

<u>Acknowledgements</u>

I would like to thank all those who have contributed to my Tai Chi/Chi Kung journey over the years and those yet to come as I am sure my journey isn't over yet. Special thanks to Master Chu King Hungs' School in Notting hill where I began my training, John Solagbade (now a Chen master) who was my interim instructor before going to Master John Dings' Academy of Tai Chi Chuan where I completed my instructor training. The College of Elemental Chi Kung in London where I qualified as an instructor and all those people who have come along to the Studio to train with me. A thank you to my partner Val who encouraged me to take my Chi Kung training further when I found myself at a bit of a spiritual and emotional impasse. I was also privileged to spend many years with Lesley and three sons Lee, Paul and Gary who put up with me when sometimes my training must have seemed a bit obsessive.
I am now the proud Grandfather to Iona, Finn, Chloe and Aimie and as such would like to dedicate this book to them and the future.

More information about Dave Allen, classes and workshops at the Tai Chi Studio can be found at www.thebalancedpath.co.uk

Email daveallen@thebalancedpath.co.uk

Printed in Great Britain
by Amazon

46421261R00046